Pitcher Plants

The Elegant Insect Traps

Pitcher Plants

The Elegant Insect Traps

written and illustrated
by Carol Lerner

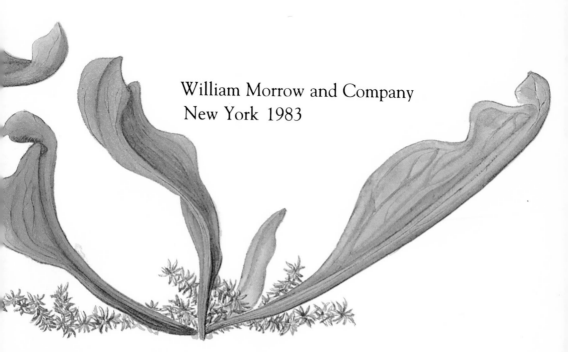

William Morrow and Company
New York 1983

Printed in the United States of America.

10 9 8 7 6 5 4 3 2 1

Library of Congress Cataloging in Publication Data

Lerner, Carol.   Pitcher plants.
Includes Index. Summary: Paintings, drawings, and text depict the species of plant known as pitcher
plants, which eat insects to survive. 1. Pitcher plants—Juvenile literature. [1. Pitcher plants. 2.
Insectivorous plants] I. Title   QK917.L47   1982   583'.121   82-12514
ISBN 0-688-01717-7
ISBN 0-688-01718-5 (lib. bdg.)

For
Chuck Nelson

The author thanks Rob Gardner,
Curator, North Carolina Botanical Garden,
for his generous help and counsel.

Contents

Plants of Prey

The land is flat and monotonous, a lonely corner of coastal plain in the southeastern United States. The air is hot and quiet under a bright noon sun. Now and then the drill of a woodpecker clatters high in the trees to break the stillness.

A narrow road leads through miles of pine trees— not forests but cultivated pine plantations. These trees stand tall and rigid, each one at the same height, planted in long straight rows. The pine needles in the treetops shade the ground below, leaving the stiff tree trunks in gloomy shadow.

Where the plantation ends nature sprawls at ease, drenched in full sun. A low, grassy growth covers the ground, but the dense green is spattered with the pinks, whites, and yellows of fragrant wildflowers. The field is open except for a few tall pines.

At the edges of the field the land dips, the ground becomes soggy, and some strange forms of vegetation stand out from among the grasses. These plants shoot up tall and sleek and are as high as the grasses. Their leaves are pale green and yellow marked with purple. They are shaped into long funnels, like golden horns; yellow trumpet is their popular name. Each trumpet leaf is topped with a round lid that hangs over the opening.

The bottoms of the narrow funnel leaves are filled wih something dark, wet, and bad smelling. A few struggling insects flap around on the surface. They are not there by accident. These insects were led into the funnels by a series of baits and barriers that cover the surface of the bright trumpet. The leaves are really insect traps—elegant, handsome, and deadly.

Pitcher Plants

Where They Grow

Pitcher plants take their name from their unusual leaves. All of them have leaves shaped like containers, with an opening at the top and a sealed bottom that can hold liquids; and all of them trap insects.

Different kinds of pitcher plants are found in many parts of the world. A large group with hanging pitchers grows in the tropical climates of south Asia and in countries bordering the Indian Ocean. Four species of sun pitchers have been discovered in the mountains of South America, and another kind of pitcher lives only in a small area of Australia.

Yellow trumpets belong to the group, or genus, *Sarracenia*. It contains eight different species that grow only in North America. These plants live in different sections of the continent, from the frigid waters of Canadian bogs to sun-baked southern coastal areas. Despite these differences in climate, the habitats where they grow are similar in some ways.

All *Sarracenia* pitchers grow in some kind of wetland. Many thrive in bogs, marshes, and swamps, places that are soggy most of the year because the water drains away very slowly or not at all. In the south some species grow on flat grassy lands called savannahs near the coasts of the Atlantic Ocean and the Gulf of Mexico. There the topsoil is loose and sandy, but a denser layer of soil underneath prevents the rainwater from draining down very far into the earth. Since rainfall is heavy and the ground is quite flat, the surface seldom dries out. One kind of pitcher plant grows on wet borders of mountain streams.

The pitcher plant habitats share another characteristic: The soils in which they grow have poor supplies of some of the minerals that all plants need for healthy growth. For instance, in the north the purple pitchers float on bog water that is always cold. Since the chilly water temperature slows the rate of decay of dead plants, the minerals contained within the tissues of old plant structures are locked away for a long time. Until the dry stems and leaves finally decompose, these minerals are not available to be used again by the living plants in the habitat. On the southern coastal plains, where the richest collections of pitcher plants grow, the sandy earth is also poor in minerals. Heavy rains wash away still more of the nutrients in the soil.

How can the pitcher plants flourish in these unfavorable places where normal plant life is so difficult? Their success is linked to the leaf traps that catch insects and use them to feed the plant.

In general, pitchers are no different from other green plants in the way that they make food. They take in water with dissolved minerals from the ground and carbon dioxide from the air. Their leaves contain chlorophyll. In sunlight the chlorophyll combines these materials into food for the plant's life and growth.

Unlike most other plants, however, the pitchers can draw upon another source of minerals as well—the bodies of those drowned insects. From their captured prey they absorb materials that are missing from the soil in which they grow. Pitcher plants will flourish in soils that are well-stocked with minerals, but there they must struggle for space with other kinds of well-nourished plants. In places that are poor in mineral nutrients the pitchers have a clear advantage over most plant competitors.

None of the eight species in this genus grows naturally outside of the North American continent, and none grows south of the borders of the United

States. Only one, the purple pitcher plant, is found over a very large area that has great contrasts in climate. Purple pitchers survive in the frozen winters of the northeastern and upper midwestern United States and northward far into Canada. Their range continues down into the southern states on the flatlands along the Atlantic Ocean, and they appear again on the coastal plains of the Gulf of Mexico.

The seven other *Sarracenia* species have much smaller natural ranges. They grow only in the southeastern part of the United States, though one continues along the Gulf coast into eastern Texas. The green pitcher plant, the rarest species, grows only in the mountains of Alabama.

The eastern pitchers have one close relative on the Pacific coast, the California pitcher plant. The leaf of this plant resembles those of the *Sarracenia* in its shape and in the way it traps and uses insects. Although this plant is in the same family as the *Sarracenia*, botanists put it in a separate genus because its flower is arranged according to a different pattern. It is the only plant in the genus *Darlingtonia*.

The California pitcher grows in mountain bogs and along cool streams in Oregon and northern

The California pitcher plant, *Darlingtonia californica*, has leaves up to 3 feet tall. As they grow, the leaves twist until the knobs at the top have made a full half-circle turn. The pitcher opening of a fully grown leaf always faces away from the center of the plant. This species can be found in Oregon and northern California.

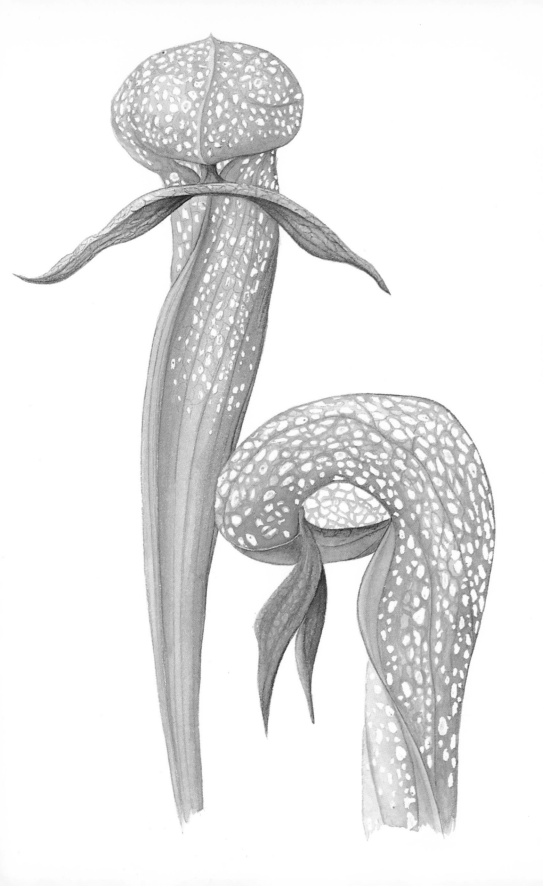

California. The top part of its leaf is shaped like a large knob over the opening to the pitcher. A long flap, divided down its length into two parts, hangs from the bottom of the knob in front of the entrance. This drooping form, like a flattened forked tongue, and the bulbous head suggest the plant's other common name, cobra plant.

The Pitcher Leaf

The blossoms are usually the brightest and most conspicuous part of flowering plants. But in the *Sarracenia* it is the leaves, with their graceful shapes and vivid colors, that are most striking. Like flowers, pitcher leaves have glands that give out a sugary nectar that attracts insects. These glands, and a variety of other devices on the outer and inner surfaces of the leaf, lure and trap their prey.

There are some variations in the different *Sarracenia* species, but the yellow trumpet plant shows the basic pattern that they share.

The leaves of *Sarracenia* plants grow in clumps, called rosettes, from a rhizome, or underground stem. The rhizomes continue to live and grow for many years, sending up new leaves and flowers each spring at the onset of the growing season. The leaves of the yellow trumpet are long tubes, standing upright and becoming wider toward the top. A hood, attached to the back of the pitcher mouth, bends forward slightly to hang over the opening.

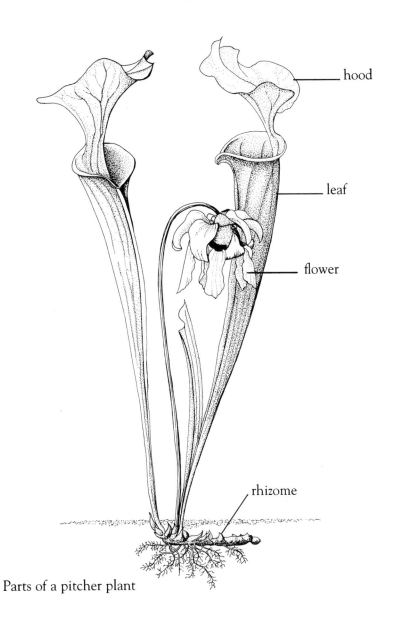

hood

leaf

flower

rhizome

Parts of a pitcher plant

The outside surface of the pitcher plant leaf has microscopic glands that produce nectar. Toward the top of the leaf the glands become more numerous and the flow of nectar is heavier. A flying insect that chances to land on any part of the leaf or a ground-living insect that wanders up to investigate is gradually led by the path of nectar toward the mouth of the trumpet. Heavy veins, more or less red in some species, and the narrow wing that runs up the front of the leaf serve as pathways for visiting insects. Both are thickly baited with nectar glands.

The inner surface of the leaf continues the design that lures these small animals toward the trap. The hood that forms a roof over the tube below contains more nectar glands and draws insects farther into the leaf. This portion of the leaf is fuzzy to the touch, covered with small hairs that offer a sure foothold and encourage further exploration. All of the hairs point downward into the tube.

The area ringing the mouth of the pitcher provides the main attraction for an insect searching for nectar. A curled-under rim, called the nectar roll, surrounds the open mouth. At the rear of the mouth a

The yellow trumpet, *Sarracenia flava*, grows in a wide band along the coastal plain of the southeastern states, from the corner of Virginia to southern Alabama. Leaves are often 2 to 3 feet tall. Usually they are pale green or yellow with red markings near the top of the pitcher, but some populations of this species show a variety of other coloration.

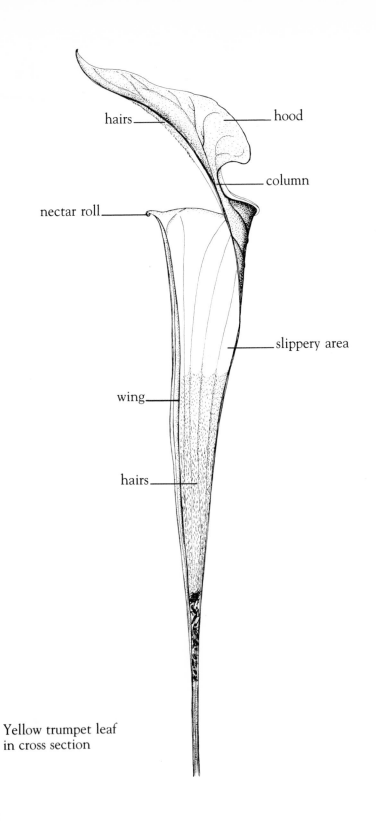

hairs

hood

column

nectar roll

slippery area

wing

hairs

Yellow trumpet leaf
in cross section

column of leaf tissue supports the hood. This part of the trumpet, a narrow zone less than one inch wide, is also crowded with nectar glands. They are so dense that this area is sometimes wet with nectar. Here there are no hairs; the surface is smooth, waxy to the touch—and slippery.

Any insect that loses its foothold while feeding at the mouth of the pitcher plant is in danger. Below the mouth is a chute, its walls covered with a shiny wax. It continues for several inches, becoming increasingly narrow. The space is so tight that an insect can barely stretch its wings to attempt flight. Glands line the walls of this slide area too, but these produce a digestive juice, or enzyme, that runs down and collects in the bottom of the tube.

When the struggling insect falls to the very bottom section of the leaf, it has little or no chance to escape. The walls here are hairy; but all the hairs are long and pointing downward, resisting any effort by the insect to walk against them up the tube.

During the growing season, this bottom part holds the fluids containing the digestive enzymes. The enzymes help to break down the protein in the insects' bodies. Most of the *Sarracenia* species produce effective digestive juices; in the species that do not, the bacteria brought in on the bodies of the victims cause a more gradual decay. The fluids produced by several of the species also contain a substance that stuns and quiets the fallen prey. As insects begin to fill the well, the plant responds by producing more liquid. The animal materials are gradually dissolved until only the very hardest parts, such as the legs of beetles, remain in the pitcher.

These digestive juices continue to dissolve the insect bodies even if rainwater pours into the pitcher and weakens their strength. In some species of the *Sarracenia* the enzymes are very powerful: One scientist reports opening a pitcher leaf and finding a snail shell that had been partly dissolved!

As the pile of partly digested insects in the pitcher grows, so does the odor. This too works to the plant's advantage, for now other sorts of insects, those that feed on dead animals, are tempted to enter the leaf. Some of these carrion feeders will also lose their foothold on the waxy slide and plunge down into the pitcher trap.

Most of the leaf's inner surface is covered with cuticle, a waxy material that makes the walls waterproof. However, no cuticle covers the walls in the bottom of the pitcher. There the leaf walls can absorb the pitcher liquid along with the minerals from the dissolved insects that it contains.

Laboratory work has shown that nitrogen taken in through the walls of the pitcher leaf is used through-

The purple pitcher plant, *Sarracenia purpurea*, is the only *Sarracenia* that grows naturally in the northern states. The curved leaves are from 2 to 18 inches long.

out the plant's system to meet its nutritional needs. Perhaps these plants also use other minerals from the bodies of their victims. Most of the pitcher species have not been studied thoroughly, and this is one of the unanswered questions about the way they function.

A few other groups of plants trap insects and use their bodies for food. Some of these, the small bladderworts and sundews in particular, are widespread in this country. The famous Venus flytrap lives in a very small and shrinking part of the coastal plain of North and South Carolina. All of these other carnivorous plants are much smaller than the pitchers, but a hands-and-knees search usually discovers one or more of them in areas where pitcher plants grow. They all live in these places for the same reason: They have a resource not available to most other plants that gives them an advantage in a mineral-poor habitat.

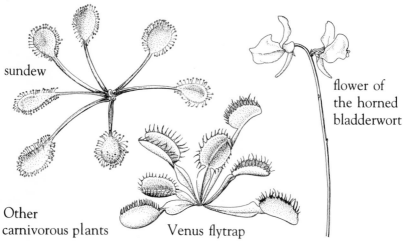

sundew

flower of the horned bladderwort

Other carnivorous plants   Venus flytrap

Some Leaf Variations

The plant with the widest geographical range, the purple pitcher, is shaped differently from the others in the genus. Its hood does not bend over to protect the tube but stands straight up behind it. Purple pitchers often grow with their leaves lying on the ground rather than upright, their round mouths open to the sky. Much of the liquid in these leaves comes from falling rain.

Just as the design of its leaf is simpler, so too is the purple pitcher's method of dealing with its victims. The digestive fluids produced within its leaves seem to be very weak. After the insects have drowned, it is mainly the bacteria brought in on their own bodies that cause their decay.

Two species, the hooded pitcher and the parrot pitcher plants, have very elaborate hoods that curve down over the mouth of the pitchers, shading them completely. A refinement in their leaves may make their traps more effective. Both plants have a series of "windows" that line the back of the upper part of their leaves. These thinner patches in the leaf wall without any chlorophyll allow light to shine into the upper part of the pitcher.

The top of the hooded pitcher leaf hangs like a dome or a cap over the pitcher opening. To an insect feeding under this hood, on the nectar roll or on the inside surface of the dome, these rear windows

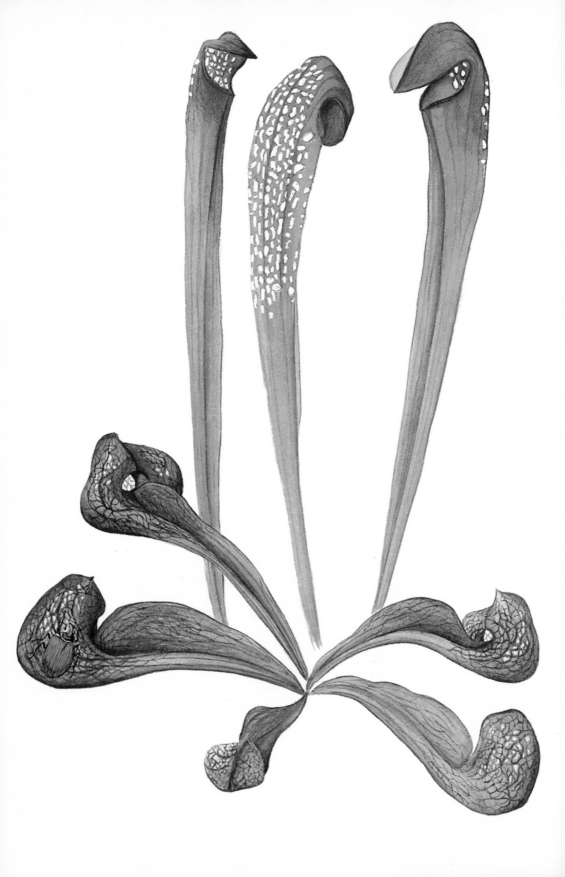

with sun shining through them would appear to be the brightest places within the leaf. Botanists suppose that insects trying to leave the plant would move toward these lights and wander from one window to the next, perhaps falling into the trap before finding the way out of the pitcher mouth.

The hood of the parrot pitcher plant is even more complicated, shaped like a round knob that comes to a pointed "beak." A narrow passage leads into the pitcher from each side of the leaf, just beneath the hood. This passage is lined with nectar glands. The upper part of the pitcher tube and the rounded hood are covered with angular windows. An insect working its way through this entrance tube might be encouraged by the sunlit interior to explore further into the leaf.

The hooded pitcher plant, *Sarracenia minor* (above), grows in northern Florida and parts of Georgia, South Carolina, and North Carolina. Leaves average from 10 inches to 12 inches long. The parrot pitcher, *Sarracenia psittacina* (below), is native in eastern Louisiana and parts of Mississippi, Alabama, Georgia, and northern Florida. Leaves are small, usually 4 to 8 inches, and grow lying on the ground.

Pitcher Flowers

Like the pitcher leaves, the flowers of these plants are strange and beautiful. All of the *Sarracenia* flowers have the same basic form. Four of the plants have yellow petals; the other four have petals of deep red. There are some differences among them in the size of the flowers, their odor, and the shape of their petals; but these characteristics show so much variation within any one species that the different kinds of pitchers usually cannot be identified from the blossoms alone.

The stalks that bear the flowers push up in early spring, usually just before the appearance of the leaves or at the same time. A single flower grows at the top of the tall stalk. The bud bends down as the time of flowering approaches. When the sepals spread back and unwrap the bud, five petals expand to hang down around a bowllike structure with an irregular edge that hangs like an upside-down umbrella from the center of the flower. This is the style, part of the seed-making apparatus of the plant. Each of the five points around the edge of the "umbrella" has a small stigma, where pollen is received to fertilize the plant. The pollen enters at the stigma and moves through the umbrella part of the style to the center, and then up the umbrella "handle" to the round ovary at its top, where the seeds are made.

The flower's own pollen is produced in the many

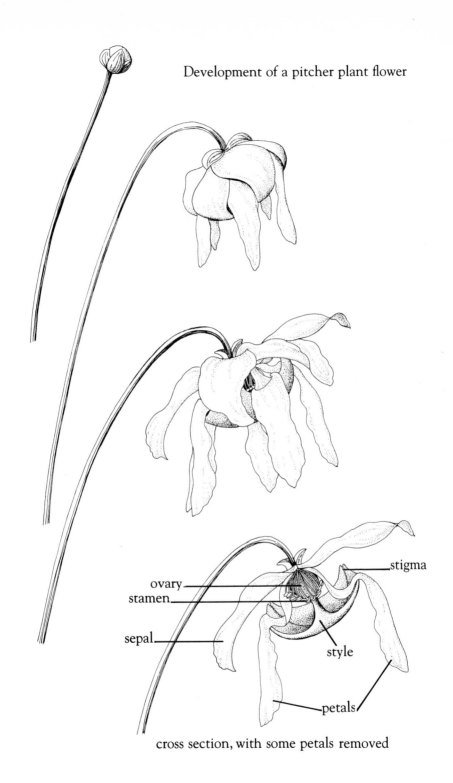

Development of a pitcher plant flower

stigma

ovary

stamen

sepal

style

petals

cross section, with some petals removed

29

stamens that hang down around the ovary. It falls down into the umbrella. After blooming the petals drop from the flower, but the tall stalk and the style structure remain standing for the rest of the season.

Pollen from the pitcher flower could enter one of its own stigmas and fertilize the ovary. In general, however, it is to the advantage of any plant if the pollen comes from a different plant of the same species rather than from itself.

Many plants, including the *Sarracenia* genus, have developed structures that almost guarantee cross-fertilization. Visiting insects, most often bees, pollinate the plants. The approaching insect, attracted by the flower's color, perhaps its odor, and by the nectar within it, searches for an entrance to the flower's center. The only obvious opening is between the drooping petals, over one of the points of the umbrella. As it enters, the insect's body brushes against one of the stigmas. Any pollen on its body from a flower that has been visited earlier will rub off onto the stigma.

While exploring for nectar, this insect becomes dusted with the flower's pollen that has fallen into the umbrellalike style. The simplest exit is at the bottom of one of the curves around the edge of the style, rather than back over one of the peaks of the umbrella. The petal can easily be pushed outward to permit escape. This route bypasses the umbrella points and avoids depositing the flower's own pollen

Entrance and exit routes of an insect pollinator

upon its stigmas. Despite this tidy solution to the problem of self-fertilization, however, the reproduction of pitcher plants is not neat and simple.

Most flowering plants will not make fertile seed if they receive pollen from a different species. If the seed they produce from this crossing of two different species is good, the plants that grow from it will themselves usually make no seed, or only very poor seed. Pitcher plants are different in this respect. They produce seed after being fertilized by the pollen of any other species in the *Sarracenia* genus; and the product of this crossing, the hybrid, also makes fertile seed.

In the southeastern states, where the largest number of species are concentrated, three or four different kinds of pitchers often grow in the same place. Crossing is frequent, and most of the possible hybrid combinations have been found in this region at some time.

Along the Gulf coast where the borders of Alabama and Mississippi meet, the ranges of two of the pitchers overlap in a large area. The white-topped pitcher has distinctive coloring. Its leaf is a slender green tube, standing tall and straight. The hood, wide with wavy edges, and the upper parts of the tube are white but beautifully lined with veins of green or red. The petals of its flower are a rich red.

Ranges of the pale and white-topped pitcher plants

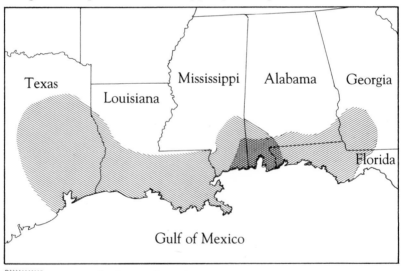

▨	range of pale pitcher plant
▨	range of white-topped pitcher plant
▨	shared range

The pale pitcher plant often grows alongside the white-topped species. Its leaf resembles the yellow trumpet's, but it is shorter and narrower. The mouth does not flare open so widely; the hood hangs more closely over the mouth. It is a pale light green with many straight red veins. The common name of this plant describes its flowers. They are creamy white or very pale yellow in color.

Each of these plants accepts pollen from the other. They produce healthy seed so successfully that sometimes there are whole fields, or hybrid swarms, of these crossed plants. The hybrid plant has a leaf shaped like the pale pitcher's, but it is white on its upper parts and has a hood with a wavy edge. Its flower is an intermediate yellow-pink color.

Does it mean anything then to talk about a pitcher plant "species"? It seems there is nothing to keep the species from crossing again and again, until there are no separate "kinds" of pitcher plants but only one large group of *Sarracenia* plants, each of them showing a different degree of mixture.

In fact, several things keep the species more or less separate. Most important is a difference in the time of flowering. In a particular grassy savannah, the yellow trumpet will usually be the first to bloom, probably followed by the purple pitcher and later by the sweet pitcher plant. Their flowering may overlap, but the main period of bloom comes at different times. With the white-topped and pale pitcher

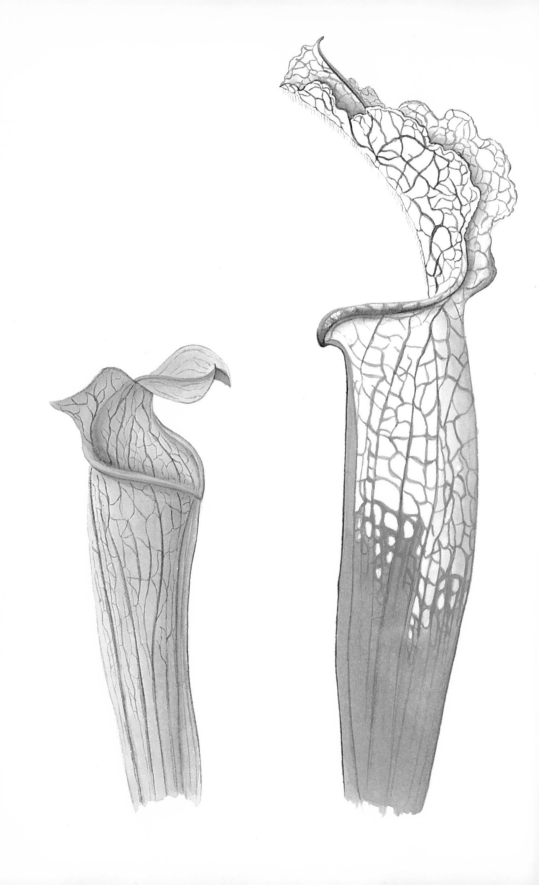

plants, this factor does not apply; both of them are in flower from early March until late April.

Insects also play a part in keeping the species separate. Some pollinators will visit only a single species as long as it is in bloom. Also, some pitcher plants tend to have smaller flowers than others, and this keeps out some insect visitors on the basis of size.

Even though the appearance of hybrid pitcher plants is commonplace in nature, the plants are not always long lasting. Sometimes they live in a field for many years and then die out, replaced by one or both of the parent species. The parent plants seem to have a vigor that is lacking in the hybrids.

Today most botanists recognize eight different species in the genus. But all living things change. Clearly the pitchers, with their easy exchange of pollen between species and their overlapping ranges, change more rapidly than most other species.

The pale pitcher plant, *Sarracenia alata* (left), grows from eastern Texas to Alabama along the coastal plain. Leaves are 6 inches to 30 inches long. The range of the white-topped pitcher, *Sarracenia leucophylla* (right), begins in eastern Mississippi and continues east into parts of Florida and Georgia. Its leaves are usually very tall, sometimes over 3 feet.

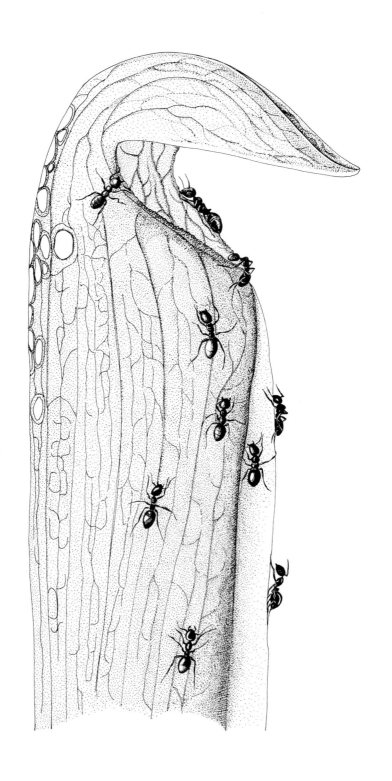

Prey and Parasites

The Victims

Hundreds of different kinds of insects are found, dead and dying, in pitcher leaves. Flying moths and wasps, creeping ants and beetles, treehoppers and leafhoppers all stumble down the slippery slide and into the pitcher well.

Some kinds of insects appear so rarely that their presence seems accidental—the odd grasshopper landing on the hood of a leaf and staying to explore within; a clumsy June beetle blundering over the edge of the nectar roll. Of course, the species of insects caught will always depend in part upon what kinds are common where the pitchers grow.

Most of the victims are drawn by the nectar oozing from the leaf. These insects include a great variety of

bugs, hoppers, flies, moths, and beetles. Ants are avid nectar feeders. Both the hooded pitcher and the sweet pitcher plant seem to specialize in ant captures. The heavy flow of nectar sends a clear signal to the ants and they come in vast numbers, often covering the outsides of the leaves as they scurry to feed all over the sugary tubes.

Other victims of the pitchers are themselves insects that feed on dead animals. In response to the odor of carrion, blowflies enter to eat the dead insects at the bottom of the tube, only to fall prey to the same trap. Spiders flock to pitchers, drawn by the concentration of insects there, and quite a few of them also tumble to their deaths.

The Plunderers

A plant that feeds on insects is not immune from being eaten by other insects. Any moth that drinks nectar from the leaf without falling into the trap, or any beetle that eats pollen without carrying some

The sweet pitcher plant, *Sarracenia rubra*, takes its common name from the fragrance of its red flowers. It grows in four separate locations: along the southeastern coastal plain, on the Gulf coastal plain, in a few bogs in the Carolina mountains, and in another small area in the middle of Alabama. The typical pitchers are small, 6 inches to 12 inches, but the mountain populations and some of the Gulf plants grow to 27 inches tall.

away on its sleek body to fertilize another flower, reduces the resources of the plant. But these are only chance visitors, and by chance they succeed in taking something from the plant without serving its needs. The lives of other insects are completely intertwined with the *Sarracenia* plants.

Small green *Tortrix* caterpillars feed on the petals and other flower parts. When fully grown, the caterpillars spin a loose cocoon around the wreckage of the flower. They stay there through the pupal stage and then emerge as small, dark moths.

All species of *Sarracenia* have thick underground stems, rhizomes, filled with starches made by the plant. The rhizomes continue to grow for twenty or

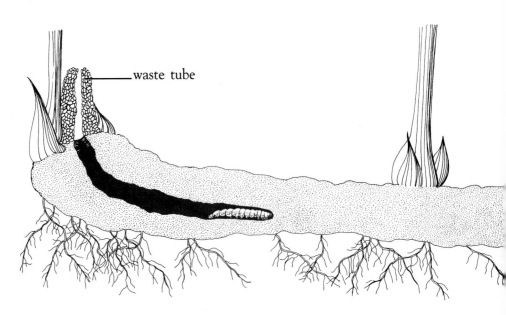

Caterpillar tunneling within a pitcher plant rhizome

thirty years and may become one foot long. One pitcher insect lives by raiding this plump storehouse. In its caterpillar stage, the insect enters a rhizome by boring in through a leaf bud. Then it eats down the length of the rhizome, making a passage through it. Waste from its tunneling is brought back to the entrance and piled up there, forming a tube that stands upright around the hole. These tubes are raised to two inches or higher by the growing larva. As the summer wears on, the caterpillar digs a special exit before it pupates in a wide part of the tunnel. The handsome moth that emerges wears the colors of the pitcher plants, maroon and yellow. It crawls from the exit hole in the fall, and the female lays seedlike

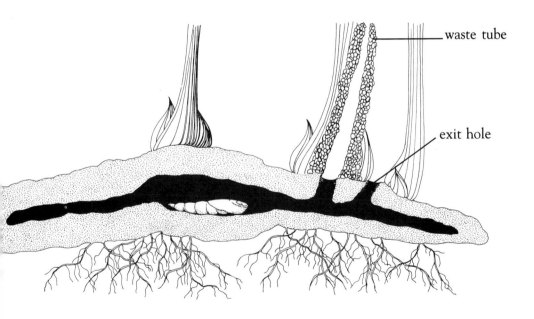

waste tube

exit hole

Pupa inside a rhizome

eggs. When they hatch in the spring, the young caterpillars eat their way into another pitcher rhizome to repeat the cycle.

Other animals invade even the leaves and turn these death traps to their own advantage. Again, some are only chance visitors. They have no necessary connection with these plants but, having stumbled upon the pitchers, they use the opportunity. Slugs and snails that lurk about the mouths of pitchers belong to this group, as well as the various spiders that spread nets across the tube and drop on silken life lines to snatch prey from the pitcher's pool. Small frogs are occasional invaders. The shadowed cranny of the pitcher, with its changing parade of visiting insects, offers obvious attractions to all of these.

None of these animals is entirely safe from the danger of the trap, and some of them never leave the leaf; but a number of insects spend a large part of their lives within the pitcher leaves without suffering any harm. They depend upon the pitchers and live only where these plants grow. Their lives are adjusted to the complicated design of the pitcher leaf: Their cycles of development and the workings of their small bodies are fine-tuned to the structure of the pitcher leaf and to the chemicals that pour into it. They live there without danger and draw upon the leaf for their own life needs.

The pitcher plant mosquito enters newly opened

leaves of the purple pitcher to deposit eggs on the pool of liquid or the moist inner surface of the leaves. The eggs hatch and the mosquito larvae, or wrigglers, swim out into the pitcher fluid. The wrigglers live in the leaf's well until they are ready to fly off as adults. They take their food from the pitcher liquid, swimming freely among the dead prey. In the northern part of this plant's range where the water inside the pitcher becomes a core of ice in winter, some of the larvae spend their hibernation frozen within the dead leaf.

Purple pitcher leaves produce only weak digestive enzymes, and the fluid is always diluted by rain that pours into their uncovered mouths. Still, the same liquid that digests captured insects seems to have no effect on these tender, soft-bodied wrigglers.

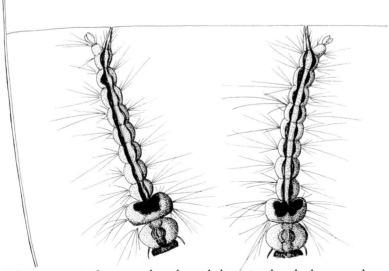

Mosquito wrigglers, much enlarged, hanging heads downward from the surface of the liquid inside a pitcher plant leaf

Several species of flesh flies also live in pitcher leaves during the early part of their lives and plunder the pitcher's catch of insects. The parent fly places small maggots on the upper part of the pitcher interior. These young fall into the pitcher liquid and begin to feed on the carrion mass. They are not affected by the plant's juices, because their bodies produce a substance that protects them from the action of the pitcher's digestive enzymes. They eat and thrive, squirming up through the growing pile of dead bodies. When full size, about three-fourths of an inch long, the big white maggots eat a hole in the pitcher wall and leave it to pupate in the ground.

Maggot, pupal, and adult stages of a pitcher plant flesh fly, all enlarged

Of all the insects that leave their young to grow within the pitchers, a solitary wasp makes the most elaborate preparations. Wherever pitchers grow within the range of this southern insect, it uses them as protective shelters for its eggs. The *Sarracenia* wasp stuffs the lower part of a pitcher tube with a plug of grass or moss. It then packs the pitcher with layers of freshly killed grasshoppers or crickets, separated by more loose wads of grass. The wasp lays eggs among the dead insects and then tops everything off with another wad of plucked grass or moss. The young develop within the sealed leaf, the dead insects providing a generous supply of food.

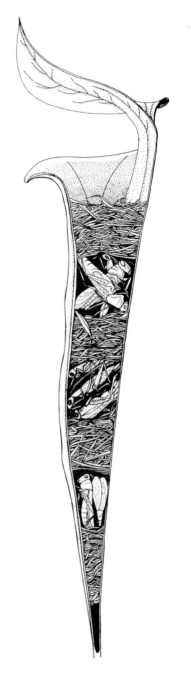

Cross section of a pitcher leaf
with *Sarracenia* wasp nests

A Special Relationship

Some insects exploit the pitcher leaf to shelter their young; the offspring of others feed on the pitchers' prey. But the insects most closely tied to the *Sarracenia* are three species of *Exyra* moths. Throughout their. lives—from egg to adult—they find shelter within the walls of the dangerous traps. Every stage of their life cycle is adjusted to the pitcher leaf, exploiting its unique structure while avoiding its hazards.

Each species of these little moths has its preferred pitcher plants. Although their lives vary slightly according to the different conditions presented by their host plants, they share the same general pattern.

Eggs are laid on the inner wall of the pitcher leaf. The small larva that hatches, transparent and half-buried in the tissue of the leaf walls where it feeds, is safe from discovery by any enemy who might search for it. As it grows, the larva will darken to a brown or a dark red, with white between the segments.

But before it reaches this point in its development, the young larva insures its own future safety by closing the mouth of its feeding room. It has two ways of doing this. The larva circles the upper part of the pitcher leaf, cutting one or several shallow grooves all around the inner surface of the tube. On a young leaf, the part above the groove soon responds to this injury by drying and shriveling, and the top of the

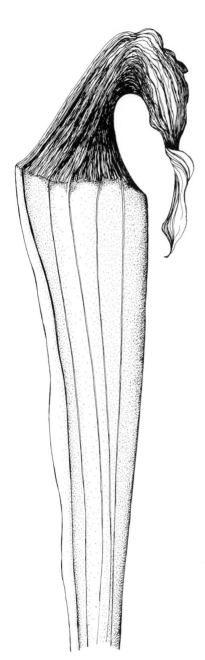

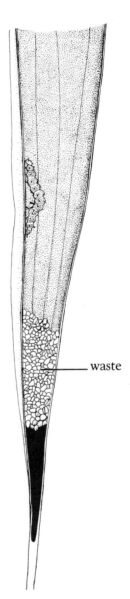

waste

Top of a pitcher leaf,
sealed by *Exyra* larva
damage

Exyra larva
feeding within
the sealed leaf

pitcher closes as the tissues shrink together. Below the groove, the leaf stays juicy and tender.

Secure in the closed pitcher, the caterpillar feeds on the inner layer of the leaf's surface. Since it never chews through the whole thickness of the leaf, the larva remains surrounded by the thinned shell of the pitcher. It stays above the fluid in the bottom of the tube, crawling about on a carpet of silk that it spins as it moves.

Older pitcher leaves are tough and the tops do not collapse when the *Exyra* moth cuts a groove in their stiff tissues. In these the caterpillar closes the mouth by spinning a fine silken web. As long as it lives within the pitcher, eating, growing, shedding its outgrown skins, it keeps the leaf surface unbroken. Any accidental holes are sealed with a wad of silk.

When it is ready to enter the pupal stage, the larva spins a loose cocoon. If the pitcher has a ceiling of silk, the emerging moth can easily leave the leaf by pushing through the web. However, it does not have the strength to squeeze out of a dry leaf top that has been closed by grooving, and it cannot eat its way out through the side of the leaf because it has no mouth parts for chewing. In this situation, the caterpillar prepares in advance for its escape. Before spinning its cocoon, the larva cuts a small hole in the pitcher wall. In about two weeks' time, after the larva has changed into a moth, this will be its exit route.

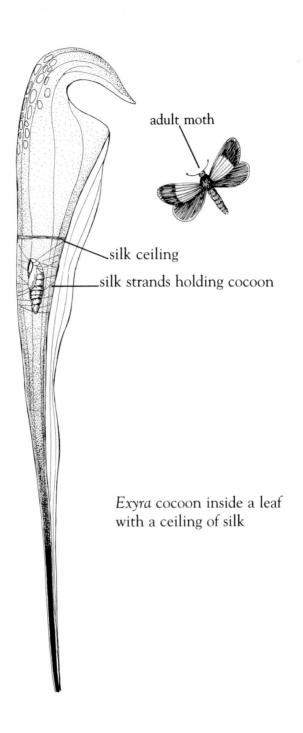

adult moth

silk ceiling

silk strands holding cocoon

Exyra cocoon inside a leaf
with a ceiling of silk

49

Even as an adult the *Exyra* moth clings to the shelter of the pitcher leaf. It spends its days resting within the tube, wings folded, always with its head toward the open end. If disturbed it backs down farther into the narrowing tube.

These little moths walk freely around the inner surface of the leaf. How they avoid falling into the trap is a puzzle, since their legs and bodies appear to have no special structures to give them a secure footing inside the pitcher.

One *Exyra* species lives in association with the purple pitcher plant wherever it grows, from Canada to the Gulf of Mexico. The shape of the purple pitcher is quite different from that of the others, with very wide, bulging tubes uncovered by the hood. The clumps of leaves frequently grow lying down, often in deep sphagnum moss with the leaves almost buried and little more than the mouths of the pitchers uncovered. The moth whose life is linked to this plant shows the greatest number of variations from the other two *Exyra* species.

This moth leaves its eggs in groups—up to fifteen on one leaf—although usually only a single caterpillar will live in each leaf. The other *Exyra* moths deposit eggs singly. Since purple pitchers grow in clumps, with their mouths close to the surface, the newly hatched caterpillars can easily scatter to separate leaves. The same kind of journey would be an enormous effort for young caterpillars hatched in the large upright leaves of a yellow trumpet or a white-topped pitcher.

After shedding their outgrown skins for the first time, caterpillars of the other two *Exyra* species have spiny structures along the wider parts of their bodies. These work like bumpers on a car. They keep a distance between the caterpillar's body surface and the wall of the pitcher and protect the larva from becoming stuck in the narrowest part of the tube. The caterpillar of the purple pitcher does not have these spines. They would serve no purpose in the wide-bodied leaf of that plant.

The most striking difference is the coloring of the adult moths. The two species living in leaves that are covered by hoods have wings of black and dull yellow. The moth of the purple pitcher is the only

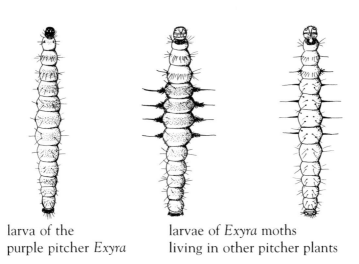

larva of the
purple pitcher *Exyra*

larvae of *Exyra* moths
living in other pitcher plants

Larvae of the *Exyra* moths (all enlarged)

one of the three that is exposed to full view as it rests within its chosen leaf. It is also the only one whose wings—yellow, purple, and wine red—match the colors of its host plant.

Occasionally these moths, parasites of the pitcher plants, are themselves targets of other insects. One small insect sometimes destroys *Exyra* eggs and a tachina fly infects some of their larvae. But on the whole, *Exyra* moths are well protected from parasites throughout their lives. The best check on the *Exyra* population is the birds, who have learned to read the evidence offered by sealed pitcher leaves with moth escape holes. They split the leaves open with their beaks and feed upon the pupae hiding within.

Epilogue

The natural enemies of plants are usually attacked by other forces in the same biological system—plant or animal—and held in some sort of rough balance. It is different in the case of human activities.

For centuries the pitchers had a measure of protection because they grew in areas that do not welcome settlement. Swamps were invaded to remove the finest trees and fields were drained at the edges of bogs, but most of the habitats of pitcher plants were little changed until well into this century.

Now, however, more and more of these lands are in use for timber production, farming, or other development. Neighboring areas where wild plants still grow are affected by the management of these lands:

by changes in the pattern of water drainage and by the use of fertilizers and poisons. Timber production requires protection from fire, but natural fires were usual in many pitcher plant habitats. Without them these areas become overgrown by shrubs and the pitchers are choked out.

People have always been fascinated by the pitchers and other carnivorous plants. Even that has threatened their survival. More often than not commercial suppliers raid the wild for their plants because it is cheaper than growing them. Gardeners too remove whole plants from the field with thoughtless enthusiasm. Some firms do raise their own stock, and any buyer who cares about the future of these plants has a duty to seek out these responsible suppliers.

Several of the pitcher species are still fairly common within their ranges, wherever suitable habitat remains. In an occasional field they make a brave and dazzling show of force. However, one species is now an endangered plant. The green pitcher, with a very small natural range, was always rare. Today it grows only in a few places in northeastern Alabama, and the area continues to shrink as more of the habitat comes under development. That it will become extinct as a wild plant seems a certainty.

The green pitcher plant, *Sarracenia oreophila,* an endangered species, has leaves 8 to 28 inches tall. Its natural range is small; it can be found only in northeastern Alabama.

The variety of forms within the plant kingdom is almost endless. A vast number of shapes, patterns, and habits of growth fit them for life all over the earth in the most diverse conditions. Even among this huge array, the pitchers stand out as extraordinary plants. As long as they and their band of insect associates continue to live in the wild, these plants will be a source of wonder. As they disappear, we will be poorer for the loss.

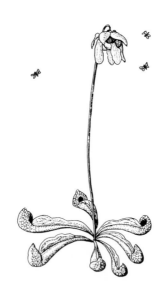

Glossary

bacteria—microscopic organisms, usually one-celled. Some kinds of bacteria cause dead animals to decay.

carnivorous—using animals for food.

carrion—the dead body of an animal.

chlorophyll—the green coloring matter in plants that changes raw materials into food.

cross (verb)—to fertilize an ovary with pollen from a plant belonging to a different species.

cuticle—a thin protective layer over the surface of a plant.

enzyme—a substance made by living cells that causes some particular chemical change to happen without itself being destroyed.

fertile—able to produce seeds that will grow into new plants.

fertilize—in flowering plants, the joining of pollen and egg cells that starts the development of a seed.

genus—a group of closely related plants or animals that contains one or more different species.

gland—a cell or group of cells that makes and gives off a liquid substance.

hibernation—the winter stage of some animals, when they become inactive and their body processes slow down.

hybrid—the offspring of parents of two different species.

larva (plural: larvae)—an early stage, between egg and pupa, in the lives of insects that change their forms as they develop.

maggot—a wormlike insect larva.

nectar—a sweet liquid produced by some plants, usually in the flowers.

ovary—the part of the female structure of a flower that produces the egg cells.

parasite—a plant or animal that lives on or within another plant or animal and takes food or protection from it without giving any service in return.

pollen—the powdery grains produced by plant stamens containing the male sex cells.

pollinate—to transfer pollen to the stigma of a flower.

pupate—to enter the stage in insect development that comes between the larva and the adult.

rhizome—an underground stem that usually grows horizontally and looks like a root.

sepals—the parts of a flower that grow just outside of the petals and protect the flower in bud. Together, all the sepals of a flower make up its calyx.

species—a single kind of plant or animal.

stamen—the structure of a flower that produces its pollen.

stigma—the part of the female structure of a flower that receives the pollen grains.

style—the part of the female structure of a flower that connects the stigma and the ovary.

Collections of Pitcher Plants Open to the Public

Collections of carnivorous plants, including pitcher plants, are on public display at the following places:

Brooklyn Botanic Garden
1000 Washington Avenue
Brooklyn, New York 11225

Denver Botanic Gardens
909 York Street
Denver, Colorado 80206
   The carnivorous plants are shown in the spring and summer months.

Fullerton Arboretum
California State University, Fullerton
Fullerton, California 92634
   There is a permanent outdoor planting in the bog of the

Fullerton Arboretum. The greenhouse collection can be seen only by appointment—(714) 773-2766.

Humboldt State University
Arcata, California 95521

Longwood Gardens
Kennett Square, Pennsylvania 19348

Missouri Botanical Garden
2345 Tower Grove Avenue
St. Louis, Missouri 63110
    The Climatron contains a small permanent exhibit of carnivorous plants, and a large display is shown for several weeks in the spring (April–May).

New York Botanical Garden
Bronx Park
Bronx, New York 10458

North Carolina Botanical Garden
U.N.C.–C.H., Totten Center 457a
Chapel Hill, North Carolina 27514
    The Garden has a large collection of native carnivorous plants and increases the stock of such rare and threatened plants by raising them and promoting their distribution.

San Francisco Conservatory
Golden Gate Park
San Francisco, California 94117
    The carnivorous plants are shown in the spring and summer months.

University of California Botanical Gardens
Centennial Drive
Berkeley, California 94720

Index

ABOUT THE AUTHOR-ILLUSTRATOR

Carol Lerner was born and raised in Chicago, receiving her undergraduate education and an advanced degree in history from the University of Chicago. She has also studied ornithology, botany, and botanical illustration at the Morton Arboretum in Lisle, Illinois. Mrs. Lerner has written and illustrated a number of books on botanical subjects, including the much-praised *Seasons of the Tallgrass Prairie*, which was named an ALA Notable Book in 1980.

The author-illustrator lives in Chicago with her husband and has two sons.